real pirates

over 20 true stories of seafaring sculduggery

illustrations by John James

text by Clare Hibbert

ENCHANTED LION BOOKS
New York

First American Edition published in 2003 by

Enchanted Lion Books, 115 West 18th Street, New York, NY 10011

CONCEIVED AND PRODUCED BY **Breslich & Foss Ltd**., London

DESIGNED BY **Balley Design Associates**

Volume copyright © 2003 Breslich & Foss Ltd.

Illustrations copyright © 2003 **John James**

Text by **Clare Hibbert**

Printed and bound in Hong Kong

A CIP record is available from the Library of Congress

ISBN 1 - 5 9 2 7 0 - 0 1 8 - 7

Contents

Introduction

Pirates have been around for 3,000 years or more— as long as there have been trading boats and coastal villages to plunder. There were sea thieves in Greek, Roman, and Viking times.

Piracy's golden age

The real age of piracy, however, lasted from around 1650 to 1800. This was before the days of steam power, when ships were slower and easier to attack. The Americas had been discovered by Europeans as recently as the 1490s. Like many other remote parts of the world, much of the region was unmapped. This meant that there were plenty of coastal hiding places for pirates.

Licence to kill

Piracy was against the law, but in times of war, governments turned pirate, too! They asked pirates to help them by attacking vessels that belonged to the enemy. These lawful pirates were called privateers or corsairs. Their payment was a share of the booty.

FRANCIS DRAKE

4

Aruj Barbarossa

A thin line

Francis Drake was a privateer for the English queen,
Elizabeth I. He made many daring attacks on the
Spanish fleet. England and Spain were at war at the
time, so the Queen rewarded Drake with a
knighthood. To Spanish eyes, however, Drake was
just a pirate. The same was true of a famous pair
of Arab corsairs, the Barbarossa brothers, Aruj
and Jheir-ed-Din. In North Africa, they were
considered heroes for their attacks on
Christian boats in the Mediterranean. They
even captured two of the Pope's galleys.
But in Europe, the Barbarossas were seen
as savage brutes.

Forgive and forget

Sometimes, in an effort to make
pirates give up their lawless lives,
kings or governments gave out
pardons. These promised that a pirate
would not be tried and punished for his
or her crimes—so long as he or she gave
up being a pirate.

World map

In the days of sail, ships had to follow particular sea routes. That was the only way that they could be sure of good winds to fill their sails, and enough islands along the way where they could stop off for supplies of fresh water and other provisions.

Easy targets

Instead of roaming the vast oceans in search of plunder, pirates stuck to the trade routes, where they were more likely to come across merchant ships. No busy area of shipping was safe. Chinese pirates inspired terror in the South China Seas, while buccaneers roamed the Caribbean, and corsairs the Mediterranean. One particular route was known as the Pirate Round because it was so popular with pirates. It went from North America across the Atlantic, down the west coast of Africa, round past Madagascar and up through the Indian Ocean to Asia.

An end to piracy?

Angry at losing ships, men and riches to pirates, governments sent out pirate-hunting patrols to crack down on the menace. Pirates who were caught were put on trial and, usually, hanged. Slowly, piracy died out. Even today, however, pirates still operate in remote corners of the ocean. They are armed with machine guns rather than cutlasses, and they plunder electrical goods instead of gold bars, but they are still pirates—sea robbers who prey on trade routes.

Where in the world?

This book covers the lives of some of the pirates who were around during the golden age of piracy. The chapters cover the areas where famous pirates operated—the Caribbean or the Atlantic, Pacific or Indian Oceans. Many pirates stuck to a particular region where they knew the waters—and all the best hideouts. Even those who sailed far and wide became associated with a particular area where they carried out their most daring attacks.

ON THE PAGE OPPOSITE, YOU CAN SEE A MAP OF THE WORLD SHOWING THE OCEANS AND SEAS TRAVELED BY PIRATES.

World map

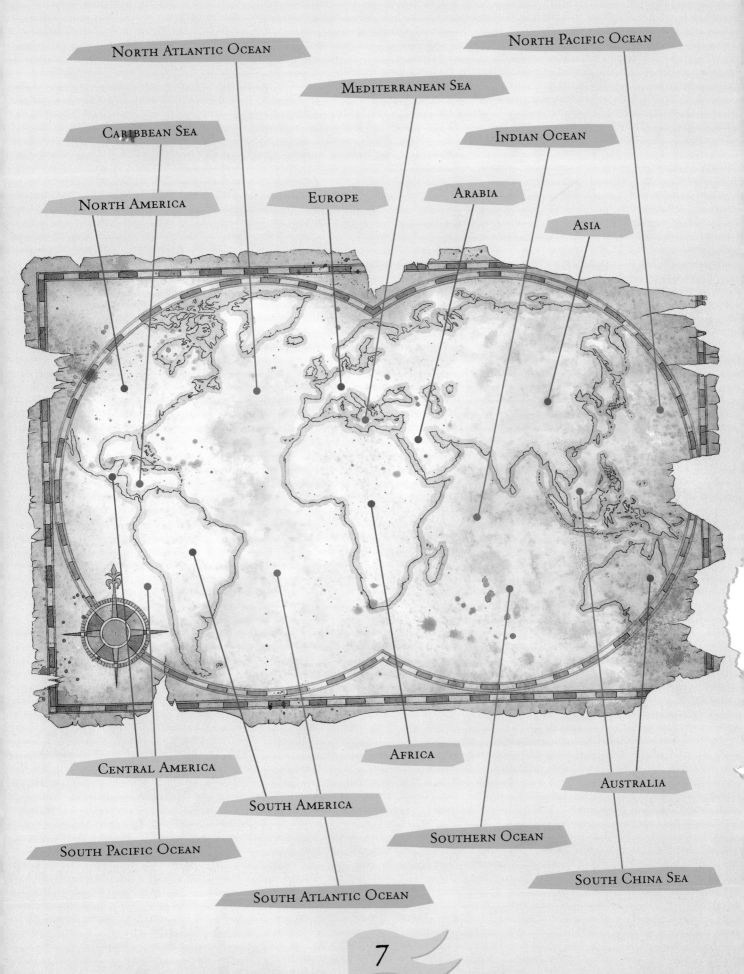

North Atlantic Ocean

North Pacific Ocean

Mediterranean Sea

Caribbean Sea

Indian Ocean

North America

Europe

Arabia

Asia

Central America

Africa

Australia

South America

South Pacific Ocean

Southern Ocean

South China Sea

South Atlantic Ocean

Spanish gold

Pirates operating around the Caribbean were known as buccaneers. These men fought fierce sea battles, and often met a watery end. The most daring of them all was Henry Morgan. His first success came in 1668, when he captured Portobello in Panama and held it for ransom. The Spanish refused to deal with pirates—until their army failed to recapture the city. Then the ransom was paid and Morgan and his men returned home 250,000 pesos richer.

In 1670, Morgan targeted one of Central America's richest ports. The buccaneers defeated the waiting army in just a few hours—but where was their prize? The Spanish had removed all the gold, but Morgan found the treasure hidden in the forest.

CALICO JACK

ANNE BONNY

MARY READ

Dangerous women

In 1720 a company of pirates was brought to trial in St Jago de la Vega, Jamaica. The captain was John Rackham, known as "Calico Jack" because of his colorful calico-cotton clothes. Rackham was not especially cruel or successful. His name went down in pirate history because two of his crew of villains were women.

One was Anne Bonny, who had left her husband for Rackham. Dressed as a man, she helped Rackham plunder ships in the Caribbean. The other was Mary Read. She had spent most of her life disguised as a man. When her ship was captured by Rackham's, she joined his pirate band.

Read and Bonny were said to be the fiercest fighters in Rackham's crew. Unlike the men, they escaped hanging because they were pregnant. Read died in prison, but nobody knows what happened to Anne Bonny.

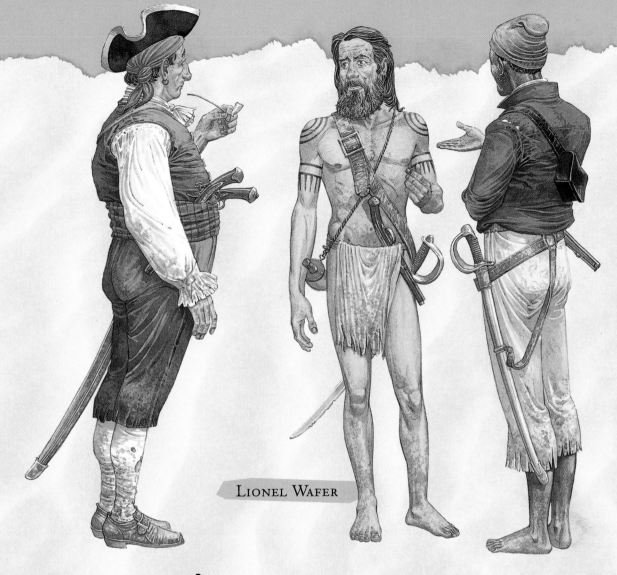

LIONEL WAFER

Pirate or Indian?

Lionel Wafer was a British surgeon and buccaneer who kept a diary of his adventures. In 1677 he joined the crew of Captain William Dampier (see page 30) and took part in many raids along the Caribbean and Atlantic coasts.

After a quarrel with Dampier, Wafer was left in the Panamanian jungle with four mutineers. Luckily they found a village of friendly Cuna Indians. The village shaman used herbs to help heal Wafer's knee,

which had been injured in a gunpowder accident. In return, Wafer used his medical skills to cure the chief's wife.

Wafer stayed with the Cuna for a while, learning their customs. Eventually, he found his way back to the coast and met up with his old crew. It took Dampier a little while to recognize his old associate. Wafer wore only a loincloth and colorful body paint—he looked more like a Cuna Indian than a buccaneer!

JUDGE GEORGE BRADLEY

The pirate judge

In 1722 there was an unusual trial on an island off Cuba. Everyone in the court—including the judge, the officers, the hangman, and the onlookers—was a pirate!

The men were part of Thomas Anstis's crew. They had decided to give up the pirating life and were hiding out on the island while they waited to hear if they could get a royal pardon.

For nine months, the band of pirates lived on fish and turtle meat. For amusement, they drank, danced, and held their mock court.

George Bradley was appointed judge. Seated high in an old mangrove tree, he passed sentence: "The prisoner should be hanged of course!"

Bradley later turned himself in, saying that Anstis had forced him to be a pirate.

"Black Bart"

Bartholomew Roberts, or "Black Bart," never wanted to be a pirate. He was forced into it after his ship was seized by pirate captain Howel Davis. But Roberts soon developed a taste for the lawless life. After Davis was shot, Roberts was elected captain. He was a brave, clever commander, who wore fine clothes and preferred drinking tea to rum.

Roberts carried out attacks around the Caribbean and also off West Africa. He captured more than 400 ships and stockpiled coins, diamonds, and other treasures. He also drew up a contract that all his pirates had to sign. Anyone who was cowardly in battle or who took more than his fair share of booty would be either marooned on an island or put to death.

In the end, a pirate-hunting ship called HMS *Swallow* caught up with Roberts— when his crew were too drunk to fight back. Roberts died from a shot to the neck.

Pirate ships & flags

There was no such thing as a typical pirate ship. They ranged from small fishing boats to elegant galleys and sloops. Pirates sailed whatever they could get their hands on—from naval vessels that they had taken over during mutinies, to merchant clippers seized as prizes. Chinese pirates sailed long cargo ships called junks, adding cannons along the deck as attack weapons. The biggest junks carried crews of up to 400 men.

Ship care

During the golden age of piracy, ships relied on sail power alone. Sails were made of tough canvas but needed frequent mending. Pirates had to be handy with a needle and thread! Another part of the ship that needed regular care was the hull. Tiny shellfish called barnacles clung to the underside, making the ship less streamlined and slower in the water. Every few months pirates had to find a safe harbor where they could careen their boat—that is, turn it on its side and scrape off all the barnacles. At the same time, they replaced any rotten wood and gave the timbers an extra waterproof coating of rope fiber and pitch.

Hoist the Jolly Roger!

Just as merchant ships and naval vessels sailed their national flags, pirate ships had emblems, too. Often, a cunning pirate flew a false national flag—it was a good way to trick another ship and get up close.

CAPTAIN EDWARD ENGLAND'S FLAG

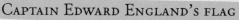

But most pirates had their own scary flag, designed to terrify their victims. The most famous was the Jolly Roger, showing a white skull and crossbones on a black background. It was flown by Christopher Condent and Edward England, among others. "Calico Jack" had his own version, where cutlasses replaced the bones. Thomas Tew's flag showed one arm raising a cutlass. Not all pirate flags were black and white. Edward Low's flag featured a blood-red skeleton. Blackbeard's flag showed a devilish skeleton piercing a scarlet, bleeding heart.

BLACKBEARD'S FLAG

CALICO JACK'S FLAG

A French corsair

Réné Duguay-Trouin was one of the most successful French corsairs. He joined the French navy at 16 and soon became famous for his daring and bravery. On one occasion, he was so keen to be first aboard an English ship to fight that he jumped too soon and ended up in the water! Another time, storms drove Duguay-Trouin to the Irish coast. Finding two English ships at the mouth of the River Limerick, he set fire to them both.

In 1694, Duguay-Trouin was captured by the English during a sea battle. He was allowed out on parole after giving his word not to run away. He soon fell in love with a pretty young shop girl, who was a French refugee. Later, when Duguay-Trouin was imprisoned in Plymouth Castle, she used to visit him. He soon noticed the way the prison guard looked at his sweetheart. Seeing his chance to escape, he hatched a plot and offered to deliver a love letter from the guard. Instead, he went to the harbor and stole a boat, which he sailed back across the Channel to France.

A fishy tale!

In 1724, there was a savage mutiny aboard a galley called the *George*. The captain, surgeon, chief mate, and clerk were all butchered. The leader of the mutiny—John Gow—renamed his ship the *Revenge* and forced the crew to turn pirate.

Gow planned to sail to the Scottish island of Orkney. On the way, he looted some ships, but their cargoes were disappointing. Two were carrying nothing but fish! Gow's bad luck continued on Orkney, where some of his men escaped and alerted the authorities.

With a warrant out for his arrest, Gow led the *Revenge* on a violent looting spree that ended when the ship hit bad weather. Washed ashore, the pirates were met by an ambush.

At the pirates' trial in London, ten were sentenced to death, including Gow. His corpse was hung on the shore at Greenwich, a grisly warning to any would-be mutineers.

MARIA COBHAM

A murderous pair

Some said that there was only one pirate who was more vicious than Captain Cobham—and that was his wife, Maria. Eric Cobham began his career as a smuggler but by the time he met Maria Lindsey he had turned pirate.

From a secret base in the Gulf of St Lawrence in Nova Scotia, the Cobhams preyed on ships laden with money or furs from Quebec. They always killed everyone on board the ships they raided. Maria's weapons were a brace of pistols and a dagger. She also used poison on one crew; she had another group of men tied up and thrown overboard to drown.

After 20 years of pirating, the Cobhams retired to Normandy in northern France and bought a large estate. But Maria hated her new, respectable life. In the end, she was as thorough in killing herself as her victims—she drugged herself and then jumped over a cliff.

"Blackbeard"

Captain Edward Teach's nickname— "Blackbeard"—referred to the long beard he twisted into dreadlocks. Before a fight, Blackbeard put slow-burning fuses under his hat so that his head loomed out from a cloud of smoke.

Blackbeard's pirate career began in 1716. Soon after, he captured a merchant ship that he fitted with 40 guns and renamed the *Queen Anne's Revenge*. For a couple of years, Blackbeard terrorized the Caribbean and Atlantic coasts.

On one occasion, Blackbeard blockaded the port of Charleston, South Carolina. While he waited for the residents to pay his ransom, he robbed every ship that tried to enter or leave the harbor. Afterwards, Blackbeard left most of his crew marooned on a desert island so he would not have to give them their share of the spoils.

Lieutenant Robert Maynard, a British naval officer, caught up with Blackbeard at Ocracoke Island in 1718. There was a violent battle. Even after he had received 20 cutlass wounds and five pistol shots, Blackbeard continued to fight furiously. When he was finally killed, his grinning head was sliced off and hung from the bowsprit. Blackbeard's treasure was never found, however, and its whereabouts remain a mystery to this very day.

WILLIAM FLY

A bag of bones

In 1726, William Fly was taken on as boatswain by Captain Green of the *Elizabeth*. But Fly had no intention of serving the captain. Within a month he had persuaded some of the others to turn pirate. Armed with cutlasses, they dragged the captain from his bed and flung him overboard. Green caught hold of a rope as he fell, but one of the mutineers brutally cut off his hand with an axe and he fell into the sea!

Fly renamed his ship *Fame's Revenge* but soon saw another he liked better—a sloop called the *John and Hannah*. While the pirates were trying to move the sloop, however, they wrecked it on a sandbar. Fly

flew into a terrible rage. He had the captain of the *John and Hannah* stripped and flogged. He had other plans for the mate, William Atkinson. No one knew the New England coast as well as he did, so Fly forced him to become his navigator.

Atkinson did not want to be a pirate. At first, he tried to trick Fly by navigating the wrong way. When that was found out, he began to turn the pirates against Fly. After Fly sent some of his men off to plunder a nearby ship, Atkinson realized his

moment had come. Fly was outnumbered and Atkinson soon disarmed him and his bunch of cronies.

Atkinson sailed to shore and handed over the pirates to the authorities. Fly and his gang were tried and found guilty of murder and piracy. Fly was defiant to the end. At the gallows, he even gave the hangman tips on how to work the ropes properly! After his death, Fly's body was hung in chains at the entrance to Boston harbor, the bones rattling in the wind.

A wicked bully

As a schoolboy, Edward Low used to bully the other boys for their pocket money. He grew up to be one of the wickedest pirate captains ever, devising horrible deaths for his victims. Once, he set fire to a ship he had plundered—but first he tied the cook to the mast. He also cut off one captain's lips and forced another to eat his own ears with salt and pepper!

Like many bullies, Low was also a coward. When one of his ships came under attack, Low did not stick around to help. Instead, he sailed away at top speed.

Low's brutality was his undoing. In 1724, after he murdered one of his own men, the rest turned against him. They threw him into a small boat and left him to die. He was picked up the next day, tried, and hanged.

"Old Crackers"

What happened to ex-pirates? John Leadstone, nicknamed "Old Crackers," had once been a buccaneer. After he gave up life at sea, he settled in Sierra Leone, on the west coast of Africa. He was part of a colony of outlaws who did business with pirates and smugglers. Leadstone traded in just about everything from slaves and ivory to pots and pans.

According to the stories, Leadstone's establishment was the most welcoming of any along the coast. Leadstone even had some cannons mounted by his door, so that he could salute pirate vessels as they sailed into port!

Places like Leadstone's were very important to pirates. After weeks at sea on short rations and with little water, they needed to know that they could be sure of a friendly supplier when they put in to port. No wonder Old Crackers did such brisk business!

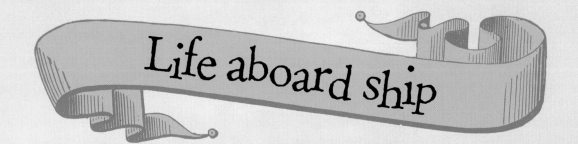

Life aboard ship

It is not surprising that pirates dreamed of treasure. Their everyday lives were terribly harsh. The men slept in cramped quarters below deck, where it was dark, damp, and smelly. They worked long shifts, called watches.

A PIRATE ON LOOKOUT SCANS THE HORIZON WITH A TELESCOPE, INVENTED IN 1608. HIS COMPANION USES A BACKSTAFF. THIS MEASURED THE SHIP'S DISTANCE NORTH OR SOUTH OF THE EQUATOR (ITS LATITUDE).

Pirates at work

The most important jobs were navigating (plotting the way) and steering. Navigators had to learn to use complex instruments, such as astrolabes, backstaffs, and sextants, and to read maps. Some of the earliest pirates sailed uncharted waters and had to make their own maps as they went along.

One of the most dangerous everyday tasks was climbing up to the lookout post, which was nicknamed the crow's nest because it was so high. It must have been difficult to grip the mast when it was slippery with sea spray, especially with a spyglass in one hand, and a fall down to the deck could mean instant death.

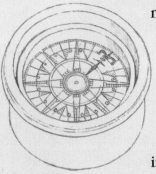

COMPASS

Trimming the sails

Many of the crew were kept busy with the sails, which needed to be raised and lowered according to the winds. On deck in all weathers, the men were sunburned or soaked through by turns. Many survived storms or shipwrecks—and many did not. Being becalmed, with no winds to fill the sails, could be just as bad. With provisions running low, the men often squabbled and grew violent.

MENDING THE SAILS

Rules and punishments

Although pirates were lawless individuals, they had their own codes of conduct: rules to obey while they were aboard ship. Along with the rules, pirate captains drew up lists of punishments. A pirate who hit another crew member could expect 40 lashes of the cat-o'-nine-tails on his bare back. Some crimes were punishable by death. Walking the plank into the sea was not as common as it is in films and stories. A pirate condemned to death was more likely to be shot or thrown into the sea to be eaten by sharks.

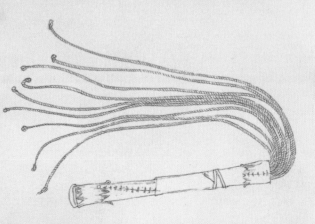

CAT-O'-NINE-TAILS

MANY PIRATE CAPTAINS SHOUTED THEIR COMMANDS THROUGH A SPEAKING TRUMPET LIKE THIS ONE.

Barber turned pirate

Chui Apoo was one of the most notorious pirates of the nineteenth century. He had been a barber in Hong Kong but then, in 1845, he took to piracy and began cutting throats instead of hair! Chui soon rose through the ranks. He became the lieutenant of a 500-strong fleet of junks.

Based near Hong Kong, which was a British colony, Chui's vast fleet terrorized shipping in the South China Seas. His pirates were armed with pikes, spears, swords, and firearms, and they treated their victims with horrible cruelty. They used short swords to chop off people's heads and sometimes decorated their weapons with hair from their victims.

In 1849, the British decided to put a stop to the pirate menace. They sent a fleet of gunships to Chui's stronghold, Bias Bay, which was just east of Hong Kong. The pirates were cornered. The British opened fire and blasted the junks out of the water. Four hundred of the pirates were killed in the surprise attack.

Chui was wounded in a later attack, but he managed to escape and avoided capture for two years. But then, in 1851, he was betrayed by some of his own men. He committed suicide while in prison rather than face the shame of punishment.

A great adventurer

illiam Dampier was an orphan who ran away to sea. In the 1670s he became a buccaneer, raiding the ports of Central America. He saw plenty of action along the Spanish Main, and Lionel Wafer (see page 11) was one of his company of pirates.

Dampier published accounts of all his adventures, which included hurricanes and shipwrecks. In 1683 he set off on the first of three round-the-world voyages. On the second of these, he discovered a new Pacific island, which he named New Britain. He also reached Australia, but was disappointed because there were no riches to plunder!

During this voyage, one of the men quarreled with the captain and asked to be marooned. The story of this castaway, called Alexander Selkirk, later inspired Daniel Defoe to write *Robinson Crusoe*. On his last voyage, Dampier rescued Selkirk—and also came home with a share of booty worth $1.2 million.

WILLIAM DAMPIER

An unlucky pirate

François Grogniet must have been the most useless pirate in history! The French buccaneer joined up with pirates in the Pacific on a mission to attack Spanish ships. But the Spanish defeated his fleet with ease. The buccaneers disbanded after quarrels.

Next, Grogniet carried out a series of raids on Spanish towns along South America's Pacific coast. Again, he was doomed to failure. Wherever he went, he usually found that other pirates had just left with all the booty! Sometimes, the locals saw him coming and hid all their valuables before he arrived.

Grogniet's men were getting fed up. Where was the gold he had promised? Most of them left him to join other, more successful, pirate bands.

But then, at last, Grogniet managed to capture a Spanish colony. Unfortunately, he was wounded during the attack. Unlucky to the end, Grogniet died before the ransom money arrived.

FRANÇOIS GROGNIET

RICHARD SAWKINS

A bold leader

Richard Sawkins was one of the 330 buccaneers involved in capturing Santa Maria, Panama, with John Coxon (see page 34). After the victory, many of the pirates turned against Coxon. They thought he had been cowardly in battle. They chose Sawkins, who had shown great bravery, to be their leader.

Sawkins decided to blockade Panama City. He demanded ransom money from its governor: 500 pieces-of-eight for each man and 1,000 for each commander. But the governor refused. Eventually, the crew became restless and persuaded Sawkins to abandon the blockade.

Sailing south along the coast, one of their first prizes was a ship carrying coins and stocks of wine, brandy, and gunpowder. Next, Sawkins landed at Pueblo Nuevo, in search of provisions. However, the Spanish had heard the pirates were coming and fortified the town. Ever fearless, Sawkins led an attack but was killed by a musket ball.

CHING SHIH

The pirate queen

Ching Shih was a tough pirate queen. In 1805, her husband died and she took command of his 70,000-strong band of pirates, the Ladrones. The Ladrone pirates attacked ships in the South China Seas and also sailed inland to plunder villages, towns, and forts. They were very cruel, and often cut their victims into little pieces.

The Chinese government tried to defeat Ching many times, but always lost. Perhaps it was because her pirates drank gunpowder before battle to help them fight more fiercely!

The Ladrones eventually disbanded after one pirate captain, O-po-tae, became jealous of Ching's lieutenant, Paou. O-po-tae killed around 300 of Paou's men then, afraid of punishment, he gave up piracy.

Mistress Ching retired soon after and the Ladrones went their separate ways. Ching spent the rest of her life running a gambling house. Paou and O-po-tae both became pirate-hunters!

Adventures in Panama

John Coxon was a famous buccaneer. In 1677, he was involved in capturing the town of Santa Marta on the north coast of Colombia. This port was where Spanish treasure ships came to pick up silver from the mines of Peru. Coxon made his name at Santa Marta with his daring kidnap of the town's governor and bishop.

A couple of years later, Coxon joined forces with other pirate captains to sack Portobello, on the Caribbean coast of Panama. Portobello's harbor was well-defended, so the pirates dropped anchor about 62 miles away and then marched overland to take the town by surprise. It was a four-day journey, and the food ran out after the first day. By the time they arrived at Portobello, the men were half-starved and their feet were bleeding. Even in this sorry state, they managed to take the town. Each pirate's share of the plunder was 100 pieces-of-eight.

By 1680, Coxon and his crew were wanted men. But that did not stop them from meeting up with more than 300 other buccaneers to plunder the town of Santa Maria, on the coast of Panama. After this success, Coxon fell out with the other pirates. Some of his men deserted him to join up with Richard Sawkins (see page 32). Coxon and his remaining followers marched across Panama's jungle to the Pacific coast, where they stole two sloops and managed to defeat the Spanish fleet.

After this victory, Coxon was a hero. The governor of Jamaica commissioned him to capture a notorious French pirate called Jean Hamlin. But although Coxon went on to seize many more ships, both as pirate and privateer, he never caught up with Hamlin. No one knows how Coxon eventually died.

John Coxon

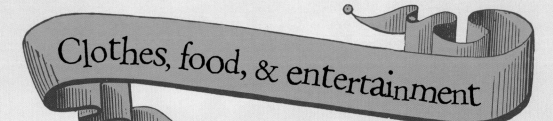

Clothes, food, & entertainment

Real pirates did not look like the ones in films. Their clothes were filthy and worn till they were in tatters. Pirates often stole clothes from their victims, so a few had some really luxurious items, such as velvet frockcoats or lace-trimmed shirts. Leather breeches were tough-wearing, but must have smelt terrible. Water supplies were precious so the men rarely washed.

A pirate's diet

The ship's cook did his best with unappetizing ingredients. A few ships kept hens for eggs and fresh meat, but more often the pirates ate meat that had been dried or preserved in salt. There was also fresh fish or turtlemeat—if the pirates managed to catch any. There were no refrigerators to keep food fresh. The staple food for most pirates was biscuits, called hard tack, that were often riddled with insects called weevils. On Chinese junks, caterpillars with rice were a delicacy. Chinese cooks also bred rats for the cooking pot!

Fresh fruit and vegetables went rotten at sea. Pirates only ate them when they came ashore or during the first few days of a voyage. Some crewmembers developed scurvy— a horrible disease caused by lack of vitamin C. Their gums bled, they were covered in scabs and their bodies grew terribly weak.

The need for water

Beer and wine were the usual pirate drinks because they stayed drinkable for longer than water. When a ship was becalmed, there was no chance of putting ashore for fresh water. The seawater all around them was no good to drink.

On one voyage, Bartholomew Roberts' crew were down to a single mouthful of water a day. Some of them were so thirsty they drank their own urine. Many became ill and several of them even died.

Time to relax

There was little for pirates to do when they were not on watch except chew tobacco, drink rum, play card games, and gamble with dice.

They had to make their own entertainment. Some pirates played musical instruments, such as the hornpipe or the fiddle. However, other pirate ships employed professional musicians to entertain the men. Their job was to strike up jigs in the evening so that the pirates could dance. They also played during pirate raids. The fast-paced music was believed to make the pirates attack more fiercely than ever!

PIRATES MAKING MERRY

Rich pickings

Christopher Condent terrorized merchant ships off the coasts of Africa and Arabia. One of Condent's early successes was capturing a whole fleet of 20 sailing ships laden with salt. Any of the salt ships' officers found guilty of cruelty to their crew was pickled in vinegar! Condent was especially vicious to Portuguese crews that he captured, because he had heard bad things about the way they treated pirates. As revenge for pirates everywhere, Condent would cut off their ears and noses.

Condent traveled widely, but his biggest hauls were in the Indian Ocean. One day, he headed for Madagascar and dropped anchor at St Mary's, a famous pirate haven. He divided up the loot and when the pirates left, the beach was littered with leftover luxuries, including spices, silks, and cloth embroidered with real gold.

The Indian Ocean

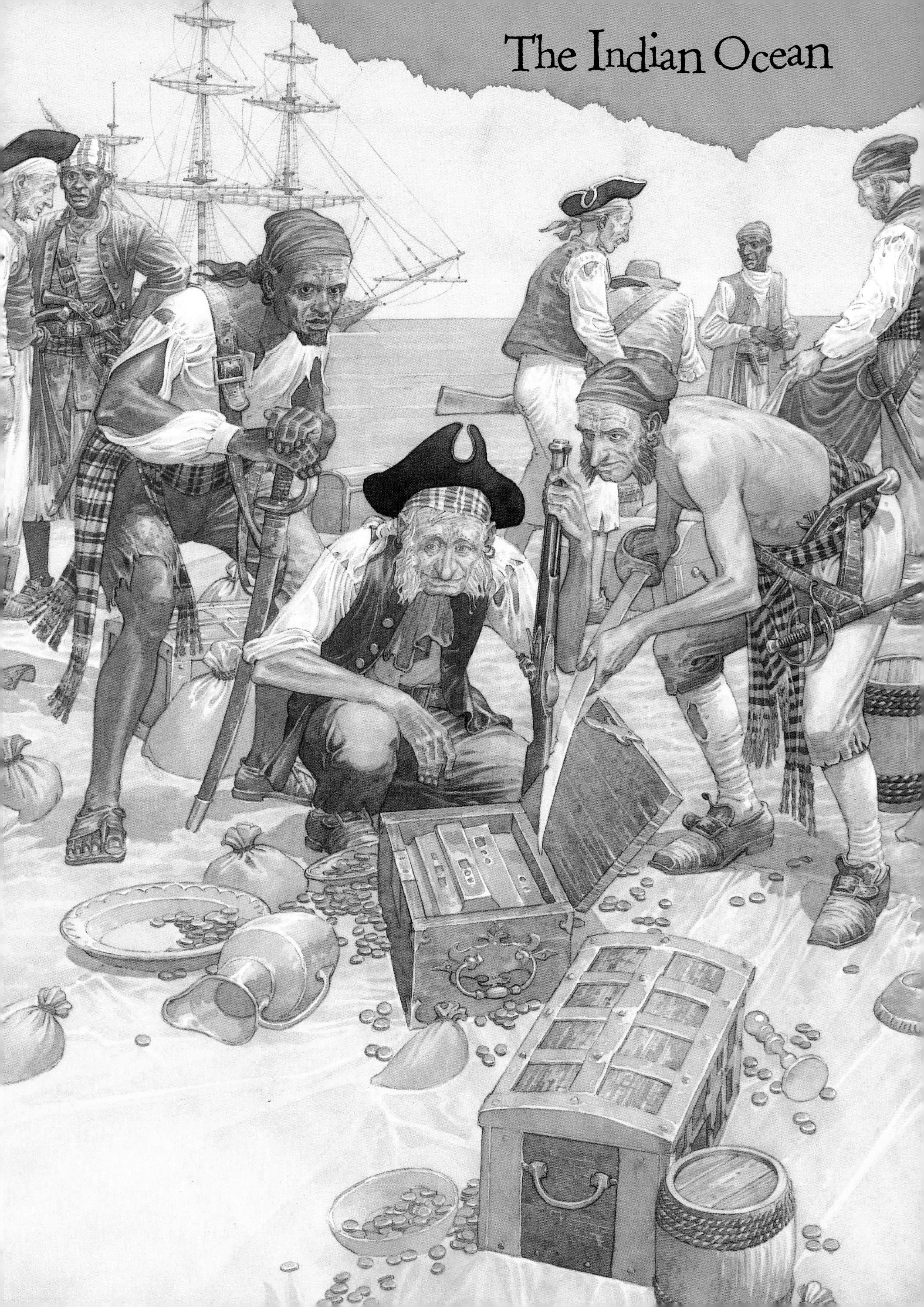

A grisly end

William Kidd was captain of *The Adventure Galley*, on a mission to capture pirates and French ships for the British king. At first, Kidd played by the rules but then, in Madagascar, many of his crew deserted and joined the pirates they were meant to be catching!

The rest threatened mutiny unless Kidd turned pirate. Kidd refused but, in the fight that followed, killed a man. After this, he did become a pirate, plundering every ship he found. His greatest haul was the treasure ship, *Queda Merchant*. Kidd's share of its booty totalled $12,000.

When Kidd returned to New York, he pretended all his loot came only from French and pirate vessels, but no one believed him. He was sent to England, tried and executed in 1701. Horribly, it took two attempts to hang Kidd: the first time, the rope broke. Kidd's dead body was dipped in tar and hung in chains on the bank of the Thames, the river that runs through England's capital city, London.

A disloyal rogue

Some pirates always showed loyalty to fellow-pirates, but not Robert Culliford. In 1690 he stole Captain Kidd's ship and sailed it to the Indian Ocean.

In 1694 Culliford was taken on as gunner on a ship called the *Josiah*. He led a mutiny, but the crew retook the ship near the Nicobar Islands and left Culliford marooned. Luckily he was rescued and, by the following year, Culliford was captain of the *Mocha*.

While he was repairing damage to his mast at St Mary's, Madagascar, Culliford ran into Captain Kidd again. Kidd forgave his thieving—but Culliford responded by stealing his crew!

In 1698, Culliford took his greatest prize, a ship carrying $195,000. Soon after, he accepted a royal pardon and retired—but when he returned to London he was arrested. The court ruled that his pardon did not count. A sneak to the end, Culliford escaped because he was needed as a witness for another pirate's trial.

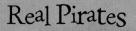

An unruly crew

Edward England was captain of a very unruly crew. One day, he caught up with a ship called the *Cadogan* off the coast off West Africa. Some of his crew had once worked on the ship and they wanted revenge on its captain, who had been nasty to them. They pelted him with bottles and whipped him. At last they put the captain out of his misery with a shot to the head.

On another occasion, the pirates tried to plunder Whydah, a trading post on the Guinea coast that dealt in gold, ivory, and slaves. But they were disappointed because the town had been ransacked only weeks before. So England and his crew sailed to another harbor. They were not popular with the locals. Fights broke out and the pirates ended up killing some of the Guineans and burning a village.

EDWARD ENGLAND

The pirates thought they might find better plunder in the Indian Ocean. They arrived off the coast of southern India in 1720, where they took several ships full of booty. However, England was having difficulty controling his crew, who were far more violent than he was. The crunch came after a fierce battle with a ship called the *Cassandra*. When England showed mercy to its captain, his crew turned on him. They left England and three others marooned on the island of Mauritius. One of the men, who had a wooden leg and a whiskery beard, is said to have inspired the *Treasure Island* character, Long John Silver. Eventually, the four men managed to make a little wooden boat and sailed to Madagascar. However, England was weakened by the ordeal and died a couple of months later.

Moghul treasure

Rhode Islander Thomas Tew was given a boat called the *Amity* by the Govenor of Barbados so that he could attack a West African trading post—but he had no intention of risking his life for a privateer's wages. Instead, he and his crew turned pirate. They sailed round the tip of Africa to the Indian Ocean.

Tew made his fortune capturing a ship that belonged to the Moghul (ruler of India). There were 300 guards on board, but they were cowardly and hid below deck when the pirates came aboard. Tew's men raided the ship's guns, gunpowder, and precious cargo. Each man's share was the equivalent of more than one-and-a-half million dollars today.

Back in New York, Tew was not only rich but famous. High society loved to hear about his adventures as a pirate. But Tew missed life at sea. In 1695, he returned to the Indian Ocean, where he teamed up with Henry Avery (see opposite). He died during an attack on a Moghul ship called the *Fateh Muhammad*.

"Long Ben"

In 1694, the crew of a pirate ship called the *Charles* mutinied and chose a man called Henry Avery, nicknamed "Long Ben," as their new captain.

Avery came up with a clever plan to raid Muslim pilgrim ships on their way to Mecca. Near the Red Sea he hit the jackpot! He captured the *Gaj-i-Sawia*, one of the Moghul's finest ships, that had staggering riches onboard.

Wealthy beyond their wildest dreams, the pirates retired. Some said Avery spent the rest of his days living like a king on a tropical island. In reality he returned to England, where he was tricked out of his fortune and died a beggar.

Avery was not a pirate for long, but his story became a legend. A play about his life was so popular that it ran in London for several years.

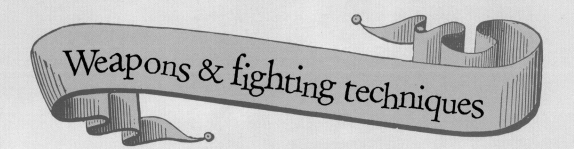

Weapons & fighting techniques

Different pirate captains had their own battle tactics. Sometimes they fired cannons to blast holes in the target ship or topple its main mast. Cannons were powerful weapons, but the gunpowder could be a problem. If it became damp it was completely useless.

ROLLING BACK THE CANNON FOR LOADING

Moving in

Many pirates attacked to a terrible din of beating drums. The noise—and the sight of a sinister pirate flag—terrified the crew under attack. The pirates would sail up close and then use grappling irons to pull the two ships together. Next, they would leap across and swarm over the enemy deck, shouting threats and waving their cutlasses. Some crews put up a fight, but they were rarely a match for the pirates' savagery and fighting expertise.

Hand fighting

Most pirate weapons were stolen from previous victims. The cutlass, with its short blade, was very popular and knives were good for surprise slashes. Pirates also swung axes or sharpened metal discs strung onto ropes. Guns were highly prized, even though they were hard to aim in rough seas. They included handy pistols and long-range muskets. However, it took time to reload firearms. Pirates often resorted to punches, kicks, or bites!

Heroes and cowards

Any pirate who was injured during an attack was paid compensation. The going rate for losing a finger was 100 pieces of silver, while a pirate whose leg was shot off might receive about six times that. Pirates who had not fought fiercely enough could expect a different kind of payback. One of the punishments for cowardice was being marooned on a desert island.

GRAPPLING IRON

BOARDING AXE

DAGGER

CUTLASS

CHAINSHOT—CANNONBALLS CHAINED TOGETHER—INFLICTED EXTRA DAMAGE (BELOW)

POWDER HORN (FOR STORING GUNPOWDER)

MUSKET

PISTOL

MUSKETOON

47

Glossary

astrolabe *(p.26)* An intrument that sailors used to navigate (find the way). It could find the ship's position in relation to the height of stars or planets in the sky.

backstaff *(p.26)* An instrument, invented in 1595, that sailors used to find out where they were at sea. Previously, sailors found their ship's position in relation to the Equator by staring at the sun and using an instrument called a cross-staff to measure the sun's angle above the horizon. Using a backstaff, a sailor could stand with his back to the sun instead, and measure the angle of the sun's shadow, which was much easier on the eyes.

becalmed *(pp.27, 36)* When a sailing ship at sea cannot move, because there is no wind to fill the sails.

boatswain *(p.22)* The name of the sailor who maintains the ship and all its equipment.

bowsprit *(p.21)* The pole that extends from the front of the ship.

buccaneer *(pp.6, 8, 11, 25, 30, 31, 32, 34)* A pirate or privateer, especially one operating around the Caribbean.

careen *(p.14)* To turn a ship over onto its side, so that its hull can be cleaned.

cat-o'-nine-tails *(p.27)* A whip with nine lashes, sometimes knotted at the ends to make the punishment extra painful.

chainshot *(p.47)* Cannonballs or half cannonballs that have been chained together. When fired, these could rip through sails and rigging—and through victims' bodies.

corsair *(p.4, 5, 6, 16)* A pirate or privateer, especially one operating around the Mediterranean.

cutlass *(p.6, 15, 21, 22, 46, 47)* A sword with one cutting edge. The blade could be straight or curved.

galleon *(p.15)* A large sailing ship, with at least three masts, that was used as a warship and a treasure ship between the 1500s and 1700s.

grappling iron *(p.46, 47)* A piece of metal with several hooks at one end, that was tied to a length of rope. It was thrown onto the deck of an enemy ship in order to secure it, so the pirates could leap aboard.

Jolly Roger *(p.14, 15)* Any pirate flag. The name may have come about because "Old Roger" was a nickname for the devil.

junk *(p.14, 28, 36)* A large wooden sailing boat, often with a flat bottom, used by Chinese pirates.

maroon *(p.13, 21, 30, 41, 43, 47)* To punish someone by leaving them behind on a desert island.

musket *(p.32, 47)* A long-barreled shoulder gun.

musketoon *(p.47)* A short-barreled musket.

mutiny *(p.45)* The rebellion of a crew against their captain or masters.

pieces-of-eight *(p.32, 34)* Large, Spanish silver dollars that were in use during the age of piracy. They were so-called because one Spanish dollar was equal to eight smaller coins, called *reales*. When the United States designed its silver dollar in the 1790s, it was based on pieces-of-eight. It was the same size and the same weight in silver.

pistol *(p.19, 21, 47)* A small hand gun.

pitch *(p.14)* Sticky, black tar used to waterproof a ship's hull.

powder horn *(p.47)* A flask for carrying gunpowder, often crafted from an animal's horn.

privateer *(p.4, 5, 34, 44)* Someone employed by a government to raid enemy ships or ports in return for a share of the booty. Also, the ship used by a privateer.

sextant *(p.26)* An intrument that sailors used to navigate (find the way) and that was more accurate than an astrolabe. It could pinpoint the ship's position in relation to the height of the Sun in the sky.

shaman *(p.11)* A wise man and healer.

sloop *(p.14, 22, 34)* A ship with its sail set lengthwise, rather than at right angles to the hull.

smuggler *(p.19, 25)* Someone who trades in goods without paying tax to the government. This is against the law.

Spanish Main *(p.30)* The mainland of Spanish-held America, particularly along the northern coast of South America. Also, the region of the Caribbean, the sea and all its islands.

Index